Pebble® Plus

ZOO ANIMAL MYSTERIES

A High-Rise Thriller

by Alyse Sweeney

Consulting Editor: Gail Saunders-Smith, PhD

Consultant: Jackie Gai, DVM
Zoo and Exotic Animal Consultant

CAPSTONE PRESS
a capstone imprint

Pebble Plus is published by Capstone Press,
151 Good Counsel Drive, P.O. Box 669, Mankato, Minnesota 56002.
www.capstonepub.com

032010
005740CGF10

 Books published by Capstone Press are manufactured with paper containing at least 10 percent
post-consumer waste.

Library of Congress Cataloging-in-Publication Data
Sweeney, Alyse.
  High-rise thriller : a zoo animal mystery / by Alyse Sweeney.
    p. cm.—(Pebble plus. Zoo animal mysteries)
  Includes bibliographical references and index.
  Summary: "Simple text and full-color photographs present a mystery zoo animal, one feature at a time, until its identity
is revealed"—Provided by publisher.
  ISBN 978-1-4296-4501-0 (library binding)
  1. Giraffe—Juvenile literature. I. Title. II. Series.
  QL737.U56S94 2011
  599.638—dc22   2010001347

Editorial Credits
Jenny Marks, editor; Heidi Thompson, designer; Svetlana Zhurkin, media researcher; Eric Manske,
    production specialist

Photo Credits
Alamy/Geri Lavrov, 11
Dreamstime/Carolyn Marshall, 9
Image Ideas, 20–21
iStockphoto/Brandon Laufenberg, cover
Shutterstock/David Peta, 4–5, 14–15; Iurii Konoval, 13; m.p.imageart, 19; worldswildlifewonders, 6–7
Svetlana Zhurkin, 16–17

Note to Parents and Teachers

The Zoo Mysteries series supports national science standards related to life science. This book
describes and illustrates giraffes. The images support early readers in understanding the text.
The repetition of words and phrases helps early readers learn new words. This book also
introduces early readers to subject-specific vocabulary words, which are defined in the
Glossary section. Early readers may need assistance to read some words and to use the Table of
Contents, Glossary, Read More, Internet Sites, and Index sections of the book.

Table of Contents

It's a Mystery

This book is about
a mystery zoo animal—me!
Can you follow the clues
to guess what I am?

Here's your first clue:
In the wild, you'll find
my herd roaming across
the African savanna.

Where I Live

North
America

Europe

Asia

Africa

South
America

Australia

Antarctica

5

When I Was Young

As a calf, I had fuzzy bumps

on top of my head.

They're called ossicones.

They got taller as I grew up.

Ossicone
Say it like this: AW-see-cohn

6

7

My Body

My big, brown eyes

see very well.

I'm always on the look out

for danger, like lions.

9

I swat flies with the furry tuft

at the tip of my tail.

I also wave my tail

to warn my herd

that danger is near.

My long legs make me
the tallest land animal.
Each of my four feet
has a two-toed hoof.

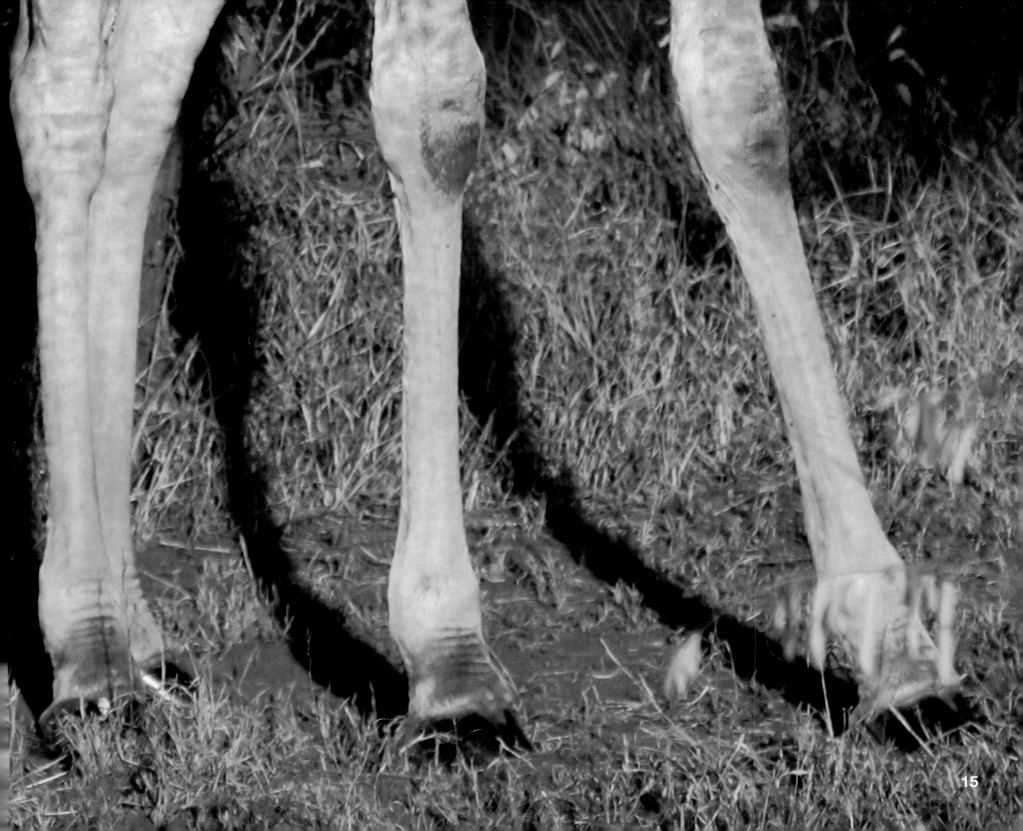

Look at my beautiful coat.

No one else looks

exactly like me.

My pattern and colors

make me harder to see.

I have the longest neck

of any animal.

My neck is 6 feet

(1.8 meters) long!

Have you guessed what I am?

19

Mystery Solved!

I'm a giraffe!

This zoo mystery is solved.

Glossary

calf—a young giraffe

coat—an animal's hair or fur

herd—a group of the same kind of animals that live together

hoof—the hard covering over the foot of a giraffe; more than one hoof is hooves

ossicone—a tall, bony, hornlike growth on top of a giraffe's head

pattern—a shape or color that is repeated

savanna—a flat, grassy plain

thorn—a sharp, woody spike on a plant

tuft—a thick bunch of hair or fur

Read More

Kalz, Jill. *Giraffes.* The Wild World of Animals. North Mankato, Minn.: Creative Education, 2006.

Lockwood, Sophie. *Giraffes.* The World of Mammals. Chanhassen, Minn.: Child's World, 2006.

Zumbusch, Amelie von. *Giraffes.* Safari Animals. New York: The Rosen Pub. Group's PowerKids Press, 2007.

Internet Sites

FactHound offers a safe, fun way to find Internet sites related to this book. All of the sites on FactHound have been researched by our staff.

Here's all you do:

Visit *www.facthound.com*

Type in this code: 9781429645010

Index

Word Count: 195
Grade: 1
Early-Intervention Level: 15